TOO PRETTY FOR PLAIN COFFEE

too *pretty* for plain coffee

POEMS BY

Tyler Hurula

WAYFARER BOOKS

ABIQUIU, NEW MEXICO

Published in 2025 by Wayfarer Books
Cover Design and Interior Design by Connor Wolfe
TRADE PAPERBACK 9781965320303

10 9 8 7 6 5 4 3 2 1

Look for our titles in paperback, ebook, and audiobook wherever books are sold.
Wholesale offerings for retailers available through Ingram.

Wayfarer Books is committed to ecological stewardship.
We greatly value the natural environment and invest in conservation.

wayfarer@homeboundpublications.com
WAYFARERBOOKS.ORG

also by the author

Love Me Louder

contents

Introduction

Tyler Hurula's *Too Pretty for Plain Coffee* is a ricocheting testament to radical self-love in a world insistent on diminishing the vibrancy of individual souls. Hurula's poems become a glittery rally cry to celebrate the messy, beautiful, and untamed aspects of life that defy the neat boxes society wants us to fit into. They weave together themes of heartbreak and joy, exploring the pain of trying to conform to molds that never quite fit— whether it's surviving a disastrous date with a cannibalistic lover or falling head over heels for a sandpaper magician whose touch both soothes and scrapes. "I personified my too much in a poem to separate myself from the reason people have left me," Hurula confides early on, creating a tender yet defiant acknowledgment of what it feels like to be too intense, too queer, too different for a world that often demands simplicity.

Within the collection, the poet reminds us that love is love—regardless of whom it's directed toward or the form it takes. Through Hurula's eyes, queer love isn't just a subcategory; it's a dynamic, multifaceted expression of the human experience that deserves celebration in all its glorious messiness. Hurula invites readers to join them on a journey filled with images of concerts, first dates, lipstick stains, and a late-night polyamorous cuddle session over a delicious glass of wine, reveling in the complexities of love beyond binaries.

One of the rawest and most striking moments arrives in a poem about deleting a former lover, where Hurula uses the page as more than a mere vessel for expression—it becomes a cathartic space for transformation. Here, the poet lists the many ways in which we die a million small deaths in our attempts to matter to someone else, highlighting the vulnerability of queer relationships and the beauty of embracing one's authentic self.

As the collection unfolds, Hurula paints the joys and anxieties of queer love with vivid, evocative language. "We kissed until lipstick smeared our cheeks into an ombre flame," they write, capturing the intoxicating, feverish joy of intimacy. The poet bears witness to a love gone too soon in the heart-wrenching poem "One More," where the form itself becomes a treasure—an embodiment of the fleeting, ephemeral nature of connection. In Hurula's tender hands, the reader is taken on a tour through the heartbreak and the euphoria of love, unfiltered by societal norms, and left with the poignant realization that we are all worthy of love exactly as we are.

—Bree Bailey,
author of *Wailing on Whisper Street*

You keep worrying you're taking up too much space.
I wish you'd let yourself be the milky way.
—Andrea Gibson, *Take Me With You*

I've Only Been Told I'm Hard to Read by People I Don't Like

I once had a thirty-seven hour first date & maybe that's the lesbian
in me, but I like to say I'm a pansy petaled with questions
like *what was the name of your first Subaru?* or *how would you describe
your attachment style?* Being with me is like going to a year-long
music festival, but it's only one song on repeat. One lover built
an advent calendar for my birthday & said the only
other person who gets an advent calendar for their birthday
is Jesus & maybe one day I'll walk on wine—I mean water,
but I like to pretend I can tell the difference between an oaky
finish & a hint of vanilla in the former. My boss said I have a gift
for being direct & it is off-putting. I've tattooed *Brutus* on my face
for all the times it's betrayed me & I've only been told I'm hard
to read by people I don't like.

I am pomegranate punch hair. Profane. Petty. Punctual—
or at least I used to be. I wear my heart as anatomically correct
rosé-colored glasses & I am pretty poet pink with jeweled
teeth & I personified my *too much* in a poem to separate
myself from the reason people have left me. I threw out the manual
on subtlety & mistake clever for vulnerable, so I clever up my feelings
& write them out & revise them. Little logic heart. I am not tender
step, more like a thump & one time I fell down the stairs & landed
with my foot in my mouth & covered in bruises & laid there until I cried
out *I'm okay* for no one but me. I won't get out of here unscathed.
I only buy lipstick that isn't supposed to smudge or fade, but the truth
is I will leave a stain that cannot be mistaken for accidental.

Before I Had a Language

for the way I love, I shared
        a twin bed with my girlfriend,
                put the whispers of a non-existent wedding

band in a box and shut the lid—a time capsule
        memory of all the things I never wanted
                to become. I collected eye rolls in a jar

next to a stack of romantic comedies,
        turned in a satire to my lit teacher detailing
                the demise of everyone who has ever said *I'd die*

without you. I had a list of famous husbands—
        and later famous wives. Commitment, at best,
                a *best by* date stamped onto every relationship.

The One a distant daydream I vowed never to chase after.

Polyamory From the Perspective
of an Anniversary Card

Of course you went straight
to the queer section—with your purple
hair pulsing, upside down pink triangle

radiating from your tattooed wrist.
There's a closet of cards glitter
flavored and rainbow wrapped,

but none for the polyamorous.
Your love is still a niche
market. I whisper commitments

of *one* and *only*—promises
you're not in the business of keeping.
You've curated a relationship

museum littered with expiration
dates. The girlfriend who wrapped
you in a brand new coat, but someone

else was already keeping you
warm. The boyfriend who wanted you
to move in, but you'd already signed a lease

on another love. You got married
knowing she'll only second
guess each new cake you bake, wonder

who you plan to serve
it to. Let me guess—
are you going to eat it, too?

You keep her gold-tied
around your finger, but you'll swipe
right on anyone, won't you?

I'll save you a sentiment in the divorce
section. You're just keeping your options
open for when they can't

hug you without getting a headache
from the smell of someone else's
shampoo. You want to play

house with new someones
anytime the music unspooling
from your love's lips becomes background

noise. It's too familiar. You think
it's okay because everyone's *agreed*
to this arrangement?

You're just cheating
with permission. I'll bet your floors
are muddled with apology

notes. You want too much.
Or maybe you're just fucking
too much. Wrong store—

we are wholesome here. You wander
down this gallery
of greetings—we both know

you won't find *the one*. I watch
you walk down the aisle toward
the arts section instead. You come

back grasping markers—the peach
of her lipstick prints, burgundy
roses blooming, his emerald eyes,

the indigo sky from your late
night drives. These colors ink
out as you alter each

hallmark. The linoleum floods in poly-
chrome pools. You rewrite my insides
to say, *When faced with one and only,*

I choose
     to believe
love exists
     in infinities.

On Loving Too Many Someones

I tell my mom I'm polyamorous
on the way to my boyfriend's

house after picking out the icing
for the wedding cake with my future
wife. She equates it to her own tangle

of affairs, can't see past the bedpost
she drove through her own marriage.

I've been living and loving
like this for years—out
in the open and I want to invite

her in. She needs time to digest
how to love someone who loves

too many someones—tells me
I am biting off more
than the people around me can

chew. I describe the time a partner
took me to meet an octopus

after mentioning I want to feel a hug
from eight different arms. Or when
another love asked me to be their partner

with a homemade lottery ticket,
and I knew I'd won the jackpot

when I decorated every inch
of the walls with cards, poems,
and songs—mementos

the people who love me
have written about me.

I didn't know that loving more
might cost me the love of someone
I thought would never leave.

I Can't Love Anyone Into Loving Me

The first time we meet, I will invite her to a show
four months out because no matter how many songs

she writes about leaving in the morning, I trust
the permanence in her sunrise hazel

eyes. I will spend hours cross-stitching a gift,
so when we're not together I stitch each memory

of them into a dinosaur—threaded into existence
against a boysenberry sky. I will read each of his novels

before meeting in person. I will never have to ask
for their coffee order, which is a trick question

because they prefer tea. I will write them a list
on all the ways they've gained my affection,

compile compliments on poppy-
colored sticky notes and handwritten cards

camouflaged behind their keyboard
or headboard or inside a book so I can imagine

them smiling in surprise. I will lie awake
counting the hours until I pick them

up from the airport. Maybe one day they'll see me
and remember what it's like to come home.

I will edit their poems until I have memorized the lines
on their forehead, or the palms of their hands.

I will add a song called *Make Out* to our playlist
while imagining our first kiss on repeat. I can't love

anyone into loving me, but if I pretend it's a trick,
I could be the world's most tender magician.

Cannibal, or My Boyfriend Dumped Me Before I Finished Writing this Poem

Lipstick is my favorite accessory and I won't take it off
for you. I wore sangria splash all over my face

      after our second date when we spent the night
      making out to a movie about a cannibal.

I wanted to whisper *eat me* into your ear,
but I was on my period and won't be served

      rare. I'll teach you the right way to hold
      my hand. I will write you love poems

too soon, and won't have the restraint to keep them
to myself. I'll send you selfies everyday so you can see me

      from my good angle, but in different outfits. I will ask
      for reassurances, compose a script on how to care

for me best. I revel in words, roll around on pages filled
with affirmations of your affections, and I wish

      I could stop overthinking your silence. I'll fill the spaces
      between us with all the things you didn't realize

you knew nothing about. Probably poetry.
Or how it's octopuses instead of octopi,

   and they have three hearts—imagine
   how many poems you could fit in three hearts!

                                        //

                  & now my crimson choked fingers drip
               as I present you with my plated heart—tender
            & garnished, reflecting the glint of your sharpened knife.

Humane

Lacerate me into palatable pieces.
Bite off my tender and beg for less bitter,
something easier to swallow. You told me
I don't have a mean or evil bone in my body,
but that's before you discovered
my backbone, encased in sinewy branches.

There is delicacy in devouring
what is still breathing.

You left me
pulsing, still beating—
called it humane.

Sandpaper Promises

The boy spoke in sandpaper
promises. Rubbed words raw
as they came out—shredded
into illegibility, like speaking
them out of existence.

While Cleaning Out My Underwear Drawer I Wondered When all my Underwear Became Period Underwear

Bundles of lace turned lunar
cycle are scattered in bright bunches
branded with all the times I thanked God

I was not pregnant.
Which isn't often because the number
of times I've had sex
with someone who could get me
pregnant is so low that my unopened

condoms are expired.
They're holy,
though not in the biblical sense.
The underwear, not the condoms—
but they may as well be because they're still expired.

And under all of this there's you.
Not actually you because it would be alarming
to have my ex stuffed in my underwear drawer,
and I'm not *that* kinky.

Your love letters—scribbled
onto cards covered in octopuses.
Scribbled so I had to squint
to read them like I have to squint to remember
I loved you. And now *squint*

looks more like a squiggle,
and I'm just playing with words
because I don't know how to write
about you. We had to break up

twice, a year apart.
You said you loved me *profoundly*
and I think I felt that, too.

I know I wanted to kiss the parts
of you that were empty, upside down.
I think I filled myself with your empty.

You scheduled a sit-down at the park
to tell me we couldn't be
friends anymore.
I said *maybe we should both walk*
off into two different sunsets

because it was so dramatic, a scene
I know you rehearsed. You didn't laugh,
told me there was only one
sunset—said we weren't understanding
each other, not communicating

on the same page. Yet this whole time
you insisted you knew the folds
in my spine, could anticipate each footnote.
But we've been writing two different books,
beginning with the love

notes now stuffed in my underwear drawer.
I almost threw them away, then thought
I should turn this into a poem, an erasure.

Polyamory Reads
[Insert Romance Novel Here]

Polyamory puts on fuzzy pajamas, pours
herself a generous glass of merlot. She settles
into the couch, blankets draped over her shoulders
like a cape. Polyamory pulls out [**insert romance
novel here**]. Polyamory loves love, and flips
through the pages and smiles as she sips her wine
with delicate lips.

By

the time

Polyamory is

halfway through,

she pinches the bridge

of her nose to keep from rolling

her eyes. She's on her second bottle of

wine. She's gathered thick red pens and circles

lines about the girl crying over which boy to choose.

Circles the time the girl demanded one boy stop talking to

any of his friends who are women. Polyamory scrunches her face

in secondhand embarrassment when the boys roll up their sleeves to fight

each other over who will possess her. Polyamory cringes when the girl

gushes over the boy as his face bloats green, and she conflates jealousy

with admiration.

Polyamory says

do it better

as she rips

out the pages, shoves whole

chapters into her mouth and swallows

them whole. Polyamory won't pretend
she's perfect for everyone, but she is sick of toxic
tropes stained red, flagging through every
[insert romance novel here]
[insert love poem here]
[insert love song here]
[insert reality tv show here]
[insert romantic comedy here]
[insert relationship advice column here]
waving proud, declaring themselves
the innocent effects of the only
wholesome
option.

the one about the girl and the closet

a girl walks into her mother's closet & says she's bisexual & the mother hands her a shirt to fold & says *you won't feel that way in ten years* & the girl walks into her boyfriend's arms & says she likes girls & the boy laughs & hands her his cock & the girl starts dating a woman & when her father asks if she's found a boy at college she gives him the woman's name & he repeats it three times, *Britta Britta Britta* & looks around like she'll parade out of a mirror, Birkenstocks first, preaching the good word of the Indigo Girls, before demanding she not tell her sisters & the girl comes out as polyamorous & her mother fumes an angry message to the girl's now wife— something about cheating & the girl tells her best friend she's dating two people & they're all happy & enamored & everyone who has only ever committed to one person at a time collectively chimes in & says *I could never do that* while 51% of them file for divorce & the best friend asks about jealousy while loving both her daughters & then ghosts the girl & the girl tells her queer friend she's dating someone whose pronouns are they & them & the queer friend laughs & says *thank God, I was beginning to think you were straight* & a primitive boy on a dating app tells the girl he's fantasizing about her & his wife & the girl is fucking tired of coming out & explaining she's not here to perform & shrugs off her validation butch & snaps six promise rings from her fingers & bites her tongue clean through & braces herself for the punchline but there is none & she bludgeons her feet against the floor & she shrieks herself hollow & last anyone's heard she's still slamming her fists against an echoing closet door

Abecedarian for a Boy on a Dating App Who Tells Me I Must Lean More Toward Female Partners and Asks What I Want with a Man

Apparently you don't know what happens when you assume
because you've just gone full ass, might as well be the moon
carved into the sky and I'm howling. I will not
deconstruct my queerness or measure my pride for anyone—
especially some blue-eyed suburban boy sniffing out someone to
fuck. I don't *lean* any way, so don't try holding me up. Your
gym membership doesn't impress me. I'm not sure what you were
hoping for, but you need a lesson in flirting. Maybe you
imagined something like me on my knees begging to
jot down all the ways your dick makes me weak, but my
kink is not having to explain how sexuality works. You reek of
lust, it's flushed on your cheeks and it's embarrassing. Don't
mistake me for a unicorn out to be hunted, horn
nailed to the wall like something you've conquered.
Offer me coffee or cocktails. Compliments. I don't have
profound expectations, but put some thought into asking me
questions that aren't about who I like to spend time with
recreationally. The answer will only disappoint you—
straddling the line between suave and a statistic.
Trust me, I don't need you for anything I can't get better from
under someone with an optional strapped-on appendage.
Vulture. Voyeur. Variations of this question have
whipped red flags through my messages so often I'm about to
Xerox copies of this poem to hand out or publish with
your face slicked like a mug shot on the cover of some
zine, hot pink type warning: *What No One Wants With a Man.*

I Went to Delete You Out of My Phone But Decided to Change Your Name Instead

forest of forget-me petaled flowers / unanswered text(s) / disappearing ink /   / unrequited love poems / there and / gone / again / faint lipstick print / lover of all things / temporary / Fridays I now have back / creative ~~partner~~ / ghost heart / breaker / phantom limb / cliffhanger / secondhand / smoke / (missed) signals / undecided / ~~friend~~ / re-evaluated expectations / head cloaked in clouds / overthought / too much of my brainspace / landmin(d) game / wanderer in a vast expanse of gray / did I even matter?

Ways to Break my Heart

Tell me I am beautiful when you break
up with me so I am certain
it is because of my personality. Replace
my name with *inconvenience*.
Tell me I'm too much.
Put pepper in my eyelids
so when I cry it burns. Remind me
of the time I disappointed you.
Paint it in bulky letters on the coffee table
so every time we're watching a movie
I see it. Tell me I'm wrong when I let you in
on how I feel—but do it while you're making
that half-smile face. The one where the corner
of your lip smirks at me while your eyes pool
with patronization. Call me at nine in the morning
to tell me you've realized this has turned into
a relationship, and you also realized
you don't want a relationship.
Text me six weeks later to tell me it hurt
to hurt me so you decided to stir it up again
so you can pour your guilt into a locket
with a pretty chain to hang around my neck.

I Meet all my Best Friends at Poetry Open Mics

for Neal

You reek of charisma. Your wit is razor
sharp like your stenciled on mustache.

My cheeks hurt every time we're together
from laughing too much. Mostly at the meat

river, or the left leaning bread, or your *duplicitous
nature*. But I looked up some antonyms

and I think they embody you better: honest,
trustworthy, and truthful. You are kind, yes,

and you *yes and* my feelings,
like when I was deep in the throws of my woes

with she who has so many names, and
you remind me that *sometimes*

my expectations could use a little re-evaluation.
I would spend any day with you in your closet.

You're a modern day Van Gogh,
but with both ears and a paintbrush

wardrobe. Thank God we're the same size
or I never would have known what I look

like in a dress with cut-out eyes on my tits.
You remind me of your favorite poem—

the days I've known you have been filled
with bright blue kicks and organ armpits.

Are You Just Being Nice,
or Are We In Love?

I traced the swirling ink on your arm at a party while making enough eye contact to make both of us blush while asking about your tattoos. How long until our first kiss?

a. later that night, in a corner away from our friends
b. 10 months from the party, almost to the day
c. when I admit I like you over text, 7 months later
d. everyday (*in my head*)

Why did you start coming to all of my poetry events?

a. to challenge me to a poetry duel
b. we're both artsy with bright colored hair so it seemed like a natural progression
c. to see if I am better at poetry than I am at flirting (*I am*)
d. you really love poetry

When did I know you might love me?

a. you bought me earrings based on the shapes you knew I was missing
b. you read a poem about your poetry crush not being about the poetry
c. you sent me pictures of you after saying you hate sending selfies
d. you added *Accidentally in Love* to our music playlist

I spilled beer on myself and tried to clean it, but ended up looking like I lost a fight with a garden hose. I pointed it out hoping to draw your attention to my freshly watered tits, and you told me you wouldn't have noticed. Were you

a. just being nice
b. not a tits person
c. distracted imagining our first kiss
d. too busy trying not to spill anything on yourself

How do you take your coffee?

a. trick question—you prefer tea
b. plain
c. pistachio oat milk latte, extra queer
d. at your kitchen table, with me

Hands

Her hands are dry—
as if the crisp air

placed too many kisses
into the soft bed of her palm.

I cradle her hand
in mine and trace poetry

shaped by the fate
lined into her wanting

palm. I imagine gods
chiseling these pathways,

carving each score. Crafting
with the same precision

as Michelangelo
when he painted

the Sistine chapel.
I stroke the swirl

at each fingertip,
notice each divot

and dip. I dance, dainty
and delicate over

the soft hill of a scar,
knowing no one can

replicate her well
worn fingerprints. I want

to swallow her whole
history, tangle up

in her bedsheets
and traverse

the entire expanse
of her hands.

The Version of Us I Almost Had

I do not cry when I masturbate.
When my vibrator dies,
it is not a metaphor.

People argue with me
over the best horror movie,
and I send them your essay,

beaming—it is how I knew
I'd be someone
to you. I flip through the pages

of the *Evil Dead 2* cross-stitch
pattern book and spend months
hand stitching the one hanging

from the wall in the background
of the selfies you still send me. I joke
that I'm either getting a dog

or a boyfriend and my life is still leash-less.
I kiss the foam from the cappuccino
off your upper lip at the coffee shop

I told you about on our first date.
You came to my poetry performance,
and when I read this poem, it was true.

One More

If I had known that was the last

kiss, I would have stopped

you on every stair. Leaped

into your arms, wrapped

my legs around you as you carried

me to your car still kissing,

crying out *one more, one more, one more*
one more one one more one more one more one more
one more one more one   *more one more*   *one more*
one more   *one more*   *one more one more one more*
one more   *one more one*   *more* **one more one more**
one more one more one   *more one more one more*   *one more*
     one more   *one more*   *one more one more*
     one more one more one more   *one more one more*
one more   *one more one more one*   *more* **one more**
     one more one more   *one more*
one more   *one*   *more one more*   *one more*
one more one more one more   *one more one more one*
     more one more   *one more one*
     more one more one more
     one more   *one more one more*
one more   *one*   *more one more*
one more   *one more one more one*   *more*

one more   one more one more

one more one more   one more one   more

          one more one more   one   more

          one more one more one more   one   more

     one   more one   more

one more   one more one morcone more one more one

          more one more **one more**   one more   more

     one more   one more

          one more one more one

                                                            one more

one more

          one more one   more   one more

     one more   one   more

one more one more one

          one more one more

To the Boy Who Traded Out My Too Much for a Life of Almosts

after Rachel Wiley and Siaara Freeman

I wish you wake up twenty minutes before every alarm,
and every cup of coffee is decaf. I wish you therapists

who get your problems almost right. I wish you
almost straight lines on your tattoos. I wish you almost

enough book sales to quit your job. I wish you unfinished
books—pages of ideas that never come to completion.

In fact, I wish you so many partners that never come
to completion. Just so much edging.

I wish you many lovers, all vanilla—people who want
to fuck you, but not like *that*. I wish you nothing

but first dates with people you don't *quite* have chemistry
with. People who are just *fine*—no sparks, only a sizzle.

I wish you almost love. Something that looks like love
if you squint hard enough and maybe stand on your head.

I hope you meet kind and boring people. People who hate
horror movies. I wish you predictable endings, almost

happiness. For the sake of the people who might love you,
I wish you never mistake *love* for *too much* again. Every time

you fall short I hope you remember
you were *almost* enough
for me.

My Dating Situation Has Gotten So Disappointing, My Wife is Trying to Give Me Dating Advice

She suggests I send a picture of our dog in a bowtie to someone I have a crush on—laughs when I say I was thinking of doing exactly that and came

to the conclusion on my own, *thanks*—but I ask what to follow it up with, and neither of us is good at flirting so we set up a photoshoot.

I tell my therapist maybe no one wants to date me because I talk too much about poetry—even my dog is named Poet

after me. They tell me to find someone to remind me what makes me *cool*, so I inform my wife she needs to write a song (about me). She delivers

with a sense of immediacy. I tell her I'd better get lucky when I invite someone over for a date. When she comes home she asks *did you get lucky?*

My friend tells me the guy I'm talking to looks like my wife and she delights in teasing me for having a *type*. I wrap my arms around her from behind

when I come home from another mediocre date and she smiles as I watch us from over her shoulder. I ask her what she sees in someone so messy,

and she tells me *a little mess is nothing against a forever timeline*, and I know if I am never loved by anyone else, I will have always gotten lucky   in love.

Poems I Refuse to Write

Another love poem to the unexplored
possibility of someone who will disappoint me.

No stanzas about the inevitable break
up after. I'm not writing about ghosts,
won't wrap them in my bed sheet and stop
in the middle of a li—

The one where I'm gushing over
the page, scarlet and sticky, and I can't see
through the thick, clotted carnage.

The one where I'm starved, but the kink
club is only open every other Thursday
and I can't keep my days straight,
so I go next door where they only serve
vanilla flavored ice cream.

The one where I am so desperate for someone
to love me, I get a Chihuahua instead,
and she growls every time I reach for comfort
in her fur and she bites holes in my fingers.

I refuse to write the poem where I tell myself
I know better, and jump off the bridge anyway
because I've watched myself do it before.

My Period

doesn't cover her mouth when she coughs,
blood clotting out of her crooked
smile. Says if I don't want her to flare
into a ruby beacon I should do something—

fast. I make her a silicone offering. She swallows
the cup and hiccups. Bangs on the door
of my abdomen with spiked knuckles.
She doesn't wait for an invitation—shoves

her way in on a semi-regular basis. Patron
Saint of the Unwanted and Empty(ing).
She steals all the chocolate, crinkles
their shimmery wrappers into the couch

cushions. She gets drunk on cheap tequila
and sobs while scrolling through pictures
of her exes. She wears a cherry tiara, invites
everyone who's ever been inside her to come

over to watch a horror movie (a slasher),
but each one politely declines. She listens
to *Stay With Me* on repeat, screams
when she's tired, but won't take a nap.

She keeps me awake with her snoring,
drools scarlet stains into my sheets, snorts
when she laughs. She never cuts her nails
and refuses to take a bath. She doesn't take off

her shoes and puts her feet on the couch.
She grins and watches me scramble
to please her. Every time I sigh she smirks
and reminds me, *don't you know I'm a miracle?*

Polyamory as Final Girl

Polyamory files her nails into sharp edges, smiles barbed wire
as her own possessed hand drags her across the floor, fingers cackling,
chipping a message reminding her she's only as good as how she holds up
her *other half*. She hacks off her hand as it tries to strangle her, straps
a chainsaw to the sticky stump of her left arm.

Polyamory plays it killer cool, hair blood-slicked back, dagger
eyes pointed at the cabin door.

She has done this before.

Polyamory strode through a haunted house littered with letters carved
into the scaffolding, declaring her deviant. Hooked her clawed
fingers through the mask of a man hiding in the shadows, proclaiming
she can sleep with any *woman* she wants, as long as she only commits to him.

She gouged her way through a graveyard, slipped through the dirt
into a cave crowded with coal-eyed ghouls grasping at her. Beady blind
eyes unblinking as they shout sermons on her descent past any hope
of morality.

Polyamory answers the phone, friend calling from the other room, ghost
faced and frantic, screaming at her for the way she loves—demanding
she choose just one.

Polyamory has been blood-stained villain by the people eagerly awaiting each sequel, rooting for a fatal misstep, battered eye, hammered heartstrings. Voyeurs gaze, call her *entertainment*, call her *confused*, saying *I'd never choose to be in your shoes*, and she stays vigilant, thrust into this violent loop

when all she wanted was a simple existence.

Predictably Unpunctual

Your sense of time is a delirious delusion.
More like a suggestion—an hourglass
        tipped on its side. We have two separate
        alarms set for the same time because I can

            watch you—literally eyes-on-
                your-finger-on-your-phone watch

                you, and it still somehow goes off two
            hours after we're supposed to be up.

        I used to be able to convince you to go
        to bed early—like 8 PM early because
you didn't bother to look at the clock.
You also assumed I am a *reasonable*

human who goes to bed at a *reasonable*
time. And I do—we just have different

        definitions of both *reasonable*
        and *time*. I could write

            an entire romance novel in the space
                it takes you to complete your bedtime
                routine. After eight years I still don't
            understand how it takes you so long.

        However, I know tomorrow when both
        our phones sing us out of our slumber,

your sweet sleepy smile will remind me
love isn't constrained to a schedule.

Her Lover's Teeth Leave a Bruise

It is black, blue, and monstrous.
Peering from beneath the soft
edge of her t-shirt. This Rorschach

bitten into her, blood ink
pooled under the breathless

layer of her skin. I try to remember
love isn't a scarcity,
even when someone you love

also loves
someone else.

I'd learned this in polyamory
class. There's no actual
class. The antithesis

of jealousy. Only she was there
with me wrapping

her green ivy spikes
through my bloodstream, screaming.
And then I'm picturing her lover's

silk black hair and she is wrapping
herself around my wife

from on top of her lap. I see her teeth
and she is laughing. The insides
of her lips are painted

with merlot, blooming.
Lipstick printing poppies

down
her
neck,

and I can hear their breath
as they fog the windows

while my peeking plants blush.
And now I am pulled back. I rewrite
this fight. Love is not a mono-fits-all

label and now when jealousy comes,
she whispers. I welcome her to remind

me that love is infinite,
and we love in multitudes.
We are *only* better

for it, and I see this in the soft spot
of her arm where there was once a bruise.

Glitter and Lipstick

I always ask a new lover
for their opinions on glitter,
kind of like kissing with lipstick on—
I look great with lipstick smirks
my bearded lover, pomegranate pink
clinging to the hairs on his upper
lip. My butch lover hates lipstick,
but wore it once when I was more salt
than smile. I picked the shade, cranberry
stiletto paired with my raspberry soiree.
We kissed until lipstick smeared
our cheeks into an ombre flame.
Glitter doesn't dull or fade. Loud,
unflinching, it sticks in the corners
of my smile, the bedsheets, and entwined
between the folded fingers of lovers.
Sparkle traced into creases, the gift
of my shine. Glitter and lipstick
are not for everyone—

                    and neither am I.

Instead of Blood it's Glitter

I offered him my heart studded
in glitter and now all I can imagine
is his shoe pressing onto my aorta until it leaks
out shiny clumps until his other shoe drops,
stomps down and I'm hemorrhaging—
but it's gay because there's so much glitter.

It's stuck in my eyelids and it drips
down my face, pools in the bed
of my palms. It flows out of my toenails
so I leave luminous footprints. I love
the way it lingers, stuck inside every crevice
so when the light hits just right, it shimmers.
He used to leave

blemished with specks
tinged on his cheeks, clinging
to his eyelashes. He was surprised
when I told him, asked why I never pointed
it out. I thought he'd notice the pieces of me
grasping. Tenacious. I imagine him years
from now, still shaking out glitter
from pillowcases, discovering it scattered
under couch cushions, catching a glimpse
of my ghost—whispering glimmers
of what we almost created.

What's Left

Maybe I should stop
writing about glitter—
but sometimes I wonder

if it's the only proof
still clinging to what's left
of us. Do you miss

the sparkle of my eye
shadow? Golden branded
butterfly kisses fluttered

onto your gilded cheeks.
I guess I just like shiny things
that stay. Like a shimmery

permanence, or a luster
memento of everything
I've loved enough to touch.

things i haven't figured out yet

underthinking   when to water my plants

coloring inside the lines   (that isn't a metaphor)

the right amount of caffeine   how to change the oil in my car

the best lipstick   how many breakup poems is   too many

how much is too much?   when to ask for help   time management

the right amount of sleep   what colors go together

and which ones don't   less pink?   when to apply sunscreen

not being afraid   of the phone   indulgence

when to say   i   love you

saying no   taking things   s l o w l y

loving myself   all the time   when to indulge   saving

money   how to look pretty   while crying   trust

falling   gracefully   swimming

becoming friends   with the snake   in my chest   playing it

cumber   cool   rhythm   taking a compliment

no   thank you   *more please*

I Have Loved You in Every Life

after Diane Lato

Once we were sisters, sticky fingered
and tickled with contagious laughter.

I was tangled in the invitation
of your strawberry hair. I cut your bangs

when our parents weren't looking,
and you rocked a mullet before

you knew you were queer. In another life
we were neighbors. We rode bikes

until crickets chirped us a symphony
in the bed of a peach-stained sunset.

I kissed you behind the playground slide
during recess, and I still feel the warm whisper

of your lips every time my cheeks flush.
Our teacher put us in time out

after we snuck into the hallway to crayon
mosaics of each other onto the wall. I used

every color in the box, rainbow eyelashes
and every shade of your favorite color

for your heart-stained shirt. You drew
me as precisely as possible, remembering

every freckle, each speck of my hazel eyes.
One time you made me so mad

I poured an entire bag of sunflower
seeds all over your yard hoping the crows

and squirrels would shit in your garden.
Now you're getting me back.

I find them carelessly stuffed
into the crevices of our couch.

I bought you a peach pie for your birthday,
sunset restless behind your wide eyes

and laugh lines. You never question
my vendetta against squirrels,

and now when I'm mad at you
I just listen to Justin Bieber on repeat

because neither of us gets his appeal,
but at least I like dancing to his beats.

I'm the one with the garden this time—
green and purple leaves stretch

toward the sky, and you are never
surprised at how well I keep things alive.

Voyeur

The sheets blushed
as they gathered

around my ankles.
The curtains held

their breath as mine
started catching.

The pillows choked
on my fingers

ruffling their feathered
necks. The bedframe bucked

a bass line against the wall
as the lights winked

off. The wooden knobs
on the dresser watched,

drawers gasping
slightly open.

Our glasses grinned
through smudged lenses

from the bedside table
as you kissed me everywhere

but my mouth.

Flamingo Sky Aubade

Stagnation slips slow,
starts all elbow

as they roll over
and we become aware

of the weight
of each other. A lazy

fumble of limbs as leg
glides over creased ocean

sheets, a reintroduction
of bodies. The tip of my ring

finger whispers hymns
over their stomach. I hum

a sigh, cheek resting
on the altar

of their chest. My palm
presses into the soft yielding

of their hip as they echo
the gesture on my shoulder

with the intimacy
of familiar ease. We blink sleep

haze, a lingering lethargy
while the sun peers

through the curtain
illuminating a halo

of entangled hair—a flamingo
sky. Thick lidded with heavy

breath we smile hazel,
more eyes than teeth.

I reacquaint myself with each
follicle, tally eyelash

wishes, graze my thumb
along jawline bristles, trace

around gauges in their holy
ear. They bow their forehead

to mine, each morning
a ritual of learning

and unlearning, a devotion
to subtle and infinite newness.

Bite Marks

My heart is an apple tree
chiseled with the initials
of everyone who's ever loved
me. Leave bite marks
on my breast
bone, but don't break
the skin. I'll gift you love
poems on apples,
I'll write you an orchard.
Nail me into your bed-
post. Let me feed you
with sticky fingers—
honey-gold and dripping.
Suck them so I get stuck
in your teeth. Kiss
secrets onto my swooning
cheeks, and don't tell
me how this will end.

Unsolicited Advice to a Recovering Monogamist From the Pretty Pink Poet

after Jeanann Verlee

When you tell your mother about your new boyfriend, don't do it a month before your wedding. When the girl you're seeing tells you she can only date you if you sleep with her husband, run. Do not wait until you notice horns hung on the wall, unicorn pelt rug on the bedroom floor. Those ropes are for hunting. When the girl with coffee eyes tells you she doesn't have time for you, believe her. Do not read her the love poem you wrote a week after you met her. When your wife tells someone else she loves them, throw a party, tape ribbons onto the ceiling fan and bake a compersion cake. When the sandpaper boy says you want to see him too much and makes an excuse not to go to your book release party—don't wait. Break up with him. When the cannibal boy texts you six weeks after he left you, don't answer. When your sometimes lover stops responding, let them go. When it feels like you're on a loop of bad first dates, re-learn to play the piano. Throw yourself a super soft princess party and make everyone write you poetry. When you fall in love, choose to keep dating yourself. Remember to keep dating your wife. When your heart aches in three different directions, bake self-pity cupcakes. Cry in your basement and watch *Pride and Prejudice* on repeat, and then get your ass to the open mic.

Another Period Poem

Fucking someone should be easy,
but I'm on my period on a first date, and I want
to negotiate a scene—but not that one from *The Shining*.

So anyway, a man walks into a bar
and I'm bleeding.

He says *I'm happy you decided to meet,* and my smile lacks
sparkle because I'm just here for the ride,
and one of us knows that's not going to happen.

I order something fruity with a tiny umbrella. My cherry
lipstick ghosts into the soft red bar-light glow. I'm straddling
his lap when I say *we're not having sex.*

He puts his hands up—a surrender, says *I'd just like to kiss you,*
and we do until I'm kissing him with my eyes open, bored
and waiting for the punchline.

An older man walks into a bar, and I'm still bleeding.
He says *I don't drink* but looks thirsty. I savor
the thought of being a novelty,
but his eyes lose focus as his fingers fidget and we both reach
for the exit sign. He walks me home, gaze lingering
on my chest, and doesn't invite himself in.

A woman walks into a coffee shop.
It's a week and a half later and I'm still bleeding.

I'm cursing the bloated break-up baggage
that brought this all on. She says *I'd like to see you again,*
and her hair shimmers in the summer sun
while my lips shrug out something noncommittal
and we hug and she leaves.

I want to feel something—will myself to exchange numbness
for lust. I'm empty and aching to be filled
by something like soft hands, but the boy made of sand
let himself be swallowed by a gentler sea.

Instead of blood I wish I could bury him
under the rough sheets of an unknown bed.

I don't want to write another poem about this boy
or my period, but I guess I'll opt for the latter
because it's the one that always comes
back.

New Names For My Sometimes Lover

Benefits, sometimes friend.
Relationship that exists
mostly on a screen. Comet
partner. Casual and not
consistent. Artist, creative
confidant. Receiver of my naked
photos. Sharer of solicited dick
pics. Cuddle enthusiast. Occasional
worshiper of my body. Limited
availability. Dwindling frequency.
Ghost role-play, translucent
and fading. Gone—
like he had never existed at all.

after leaving the movie theater the necronomicon recording plays on repeat

dead   by dawn   choked chainsaw cutting   through crimson   downpour
there is a deep shade   of bruise and you're missing it   kissing him behind
the question   of his earlobe   ropeburn yellow   battered burgundy rich

hues pool in sizzled   blood-scalped lakes   you put his hand   on your leg
squeeze his bicep as   woman   cackles   bites the eyeball   teeth rupture-
sharp as she spits   it out veiny   wiggling   you inhale gore-   filled lesions

rivering   into salt-licked   lacerations covered in promises   he   ~~liked~~ lied
about liking   the   TOO MUCH   of you   woodchipper chest   palpitate
as you exhale   sta cca to breath-quakes   what is real never gets easy

with practice   you have *practiced*   love   to the point   of self flagellation
not what you meant   when you said you were kinky   you said *tie me up*
and tell me I'm pretty   you are pretty   enough   if not   for him   you wore

white   shoes now stained ruby   no rainbows   immediate chemistry palpable
from first touch   now you're unglued   gutpunchdrunk   decidedly not
groovy   you could have loved him   you could have loved him   *so*   well.

The First Time I Masturbate After Our Breakup

I grant myself this small indulgence, empty
the side table of your books, darken
the room and sink into the middle of the bedsheets.

Let my fingers linger over the metal in my chest,
moving down, meandering through memories,
longing and earnest for desire to build,

as I try to focus on anything but
you. Which only makes me think of you harder.
I open my eyes to the empty room devoid

of you. Spread myself gentle, eyes still open—
determined to prove I can do this without you.
Exasperated and wanting to find myself wanting,

I beg myself to yield—close my eyes and we
are at the coffee shop. Lashes flutter open to your musky
absence hanging in the air, toying with my insatiability—

this ache. I love pairing pleasure and pain so I surrender.
You're here and I am squirming beneath your heavy
omission. I am a river and you're rushing between

my legs, vibrations become your fingers yearning
for where I open. I lose inhibitions, eager with anticipation.
I bury myself into a throbbing emptiness. I'm paralyzed

by the pang of absence—release consuming
and consummated. I have come
undone, ruined. Left alone to clean up this mess.

Schrödinger's Heart

I am Schrödinger's heart—both bruised & brimming
depending on who is paying attention
to me. I am a revolving door of requitement,
both bathed in affection & rendered empty

depending on who is still paying attention
& I've gotten good at writing breakup poems
bathed in an absent affection. I'm rendered empty
by the people who have not loved me back.

I've gotten good at writing breakup poems
& when I ask my lover who stays if I'm dramatic—
as one of the people that has continued to love me back,
her answer is laughter because it is obvious.

I ask my lover, the one who has stayed, if I'm dramatic.
She says I just find the biggest ways to express myself
& obviously, the answer is laughter.
I love loud, but break louder

because I find the biggest ways to express myself—
like when I wrote a breakup poem after a promising first date.
I break loud & choose to love louder,
cry from what broke & piece together

the love poems I also wrote after that promising first date.
I am a revolving door of requitement.
Always crying, but making peace with the broken pieces,
both bruised and brimming from my Schrödinger's heart.

Congratulations! We're Both Poets, and I Think I'm Falling for You

after Nic Morrison

Give me enough time to edit,
and I will write you something parading

as elegant—but not everything is a metaphor,

so mostly I'll gift you a stream rivering
through the contours of my tongue-tided

mind. We will swoon over stanzas while reading

each other poetry. You tease me for quoting
that one poet, but when you're not around

I quote you. You're my favorite

pre-dawn conversation for when I'd rather daydream
myself sleepless inside your sheets. Secrets sway

verses in the songs on our playlist because everything

is a metaphor. I could've written a manuscript
out of the times I've almost said I love

your eyes. They're gilded leaves quivering a serenade

against the grayscale sky on the day I wished I could kiss
you after I got my tattoo. Our hazel eyes slip velvet,

vary shades depending on what we are wearing

of each other's breath. Trust me when I tell you
I have always known the exact proximity of our lips,

have savored the hints of whispers teasing the tips

of our fingers—a gentle palming of the pulsing
between us. But not everything is a metaphor,

and some days I spend hours trying to impress you

with a clever response, but reply *I'm just trying
to flirt with you* because being earnest is its own

kind of truth, and I only ever want to be honest

with you. I'll compose love notes on sticky pink
paper, post them as pretty pieces of myself to display

in your bedroom. When I wake up without you,

I am only aware of what's missing. When I pick you
up from the airport and leave lipstick on your table,

it's on purpose—because everything is a metaphor,

and I will poem you a picture with ten thousand words
about you. About us. About your eyes and a daydream—
about how our lips linger before closing the distance between us.

Edging, or Instead of Saying I Love You

I want the word *love* to coat
my mouth sticky, messy

in the way it lingers until I swallow
the sound—a game of how close

I can get before the word shapes
itself out loud. I will hold

it against my teeth, mold
each letter a deep cherry red.

I'll sigh it as I bite into the side
of your neck. It will hide

hot-breath-heavy on my lips
hovering over your ear.

I will carve it into your back
the nights you make an altar

of my body. I will tease
my tongue around it, lick

around the tip—this saying
and not saying, while you drip

into my mouth. I will come
over, quiver when your hand strokes

the small of my back in the kitchen.
I will come over and trace delicate

fingers down your chest while I lay
across your lap. I will come over

and over and over until
love is the only thing left unsaid.

Do Bees Leave Ass Prints in Petals?

I'd bubblegum the sky—sun shining streamers. If I let myself be too much,
I would tell everyone I love I love them with my golden pen, aqua ink
calligraphied onto handwritten cards, cursive with hearts dotted over *i's*.
I would use my shower voice to acoustic the corners of the coffee shop
with my favorite songs. I'd tether myself to truths instead of agonizing
imaginary scenarios into existence. How much muchness could I fit
in my pockets? I'd flood them with bee-filled bouquets because sometimes bees
fall asleep inside flowers, and I want to be unashamed with my ass sticking out
of a petaled bed while I take a perfumed nap. I'd wear different jeweled
slippers every day, would dress myself in tulle and glitter. Princess
my way around the grocery store. I'd become my own fairy godmother
and grant myself milk chocolate, pistachio lattes, and pink light bulbs.
I'd never be ashamed to take up space. I would trip over myself again and again,
fall awkward and beautiful into my own outstretched arms waiting to catch me.

in which I ask for a refund on the relationship you realized you didn't want after you realized this was a relationship

I send you a venmo request
for the gas I've wasted
driving to your house & stop
writing love poems & ask my friends
to rate you—*zero* out of five stars
& stamp it onto your dating profile & forget
the time your eight-year-old daughter
said she loves me & forget you asked me
to meet her after two weeks & I say *no*
when you ask to visit me at work
after I told you I don't want to meet for coffee
I stop drinking coffee & start drinking
wine & write new love poems & delete
our text thread & send pictures of my tits
to different people & wonder
who you went with to the concert & shove
you into a few words on some pages
& crumple them up then smooth the folds
& read them on stage & revise
the poem I was in the middle
of writing & block you & now when you search
for me I'm just ~~used~~ *user not found.*

Erasure Poem from a Card I Found in my Underwear Drawer

█████ ,

███████████████████████████████████████

███████████████████████████████████████

████████████████████ Well, ██████████ We ███

survived ████████████████████████████████

███████████████████████████████████████

███████████████████████████████████████

███████████████████████████████████████

███████████████████████████████████████

███████████████████████████████████████

███████████████████████████████████████

███████████████████████████████████████

███████████████████████████████████████

███████████████████████████████████████

███████████████████████████████████████

███████████████████████████████████████

███████████████████████████████████████

███████████████████████████████████████

███████████████████████████████████████ each other

███████████████████████████████████████

███████████████████████████████████████

██████████████████████████████

Letters to Ex-Lovers, Ending in One for Myself *a matching test*

I'm sorry I broke up with you on your birthday	Sandpaper Promises
Surprise, I'm still bisexual!	Sometimes Lover
I just wasn't into your husband	Bouquet of Red Flags
I was never going to fuck you	Nightmare on Ogden St.
You were the best sex I never had	Re-Evaluated Expectations
You are one big predictable ending	She Who Has So Many Names
I loved you	Unchecked Jealousy
Fuck you	Blush Queen
You were the worst ghost	Chris #6
Thank you for being a soft place to land	Scared of a Little Blood
We wrapped the worst of us in shiny paper, disguised it to resemble something like love	Cannibal with Glinting Teeth
Your wife was so much hotter than you	The One Who Handed Me His Cock
I wish I had let you break up with me the first time you tried	Unicorn Hunter #4
You are my villain origin story	Erasure from My Underwear Drawer
I wanted you to want me more	Not-so-Secret Canadian Boyfriend
We made out until my lips were bruised	Voice of the Necronomicon Recording
My friends told me to stop dating people with your name	Washed Up Magician
Dear Me	I am still learning how to love you.

When Everyone You Love Leaves

Lap honey from each fingertip, let it rest
on sultry taste buds. Reach toward secrets spread
out on duck feather pillows. Forget your pulse
is trying to outrun you. Smash rhubarb into a rhythmic
pulp—no sugar. Paint it across your belly and wait

for the bees. Stop writing love poems
to people you've just met. They'll hollow
out your forearms with brittle teeth. Present
them with the light reflected from the corner
of your eye. Serve it with a sharp spoon.

Cut your chest open and chew on your own blue
blood. Scratch your name into every surface
until all your pens run dry, then carve
it with your teeth and your nails. Chisel yourself
into a bloody and sharpened existence.

Keep writing love poems
to people you've just met, let lipstick stain
them maroon. Tend to wilted wishes
with the bees who once feasted on the pulp
of what your body has to offer. Etch

lovers' names onto your warm tongue, taste the wisps
of fine sugar spun out and sticky—clinging
to your cavities. Plant yourself in a garden
and sleep until you feel veins sprout from deep
lesions. Wrap the roots into ribbons around your battered
becoming and continue to offer it up.

A Letter to My Younger Self About Straight Girls

Straight girls do not cross their delicate fingers
with smeared nail polish hoping for the attention
of the popular girls, whispering *pick me* when Alexa
chooses teammates for a game they do not know
or care how to play. They do not play spin the bottle
and kiss each other on the lips at a slumber party in barbie
pajamas. In a church lecture about gay people
needing to pretend they're straight, they do not walk away
focused on the realization that this means gay people do,
in fact, exist, and it's not just a *lifestyle choice*. Straight girls
do not look up videos of girls kissing while hiding
under the sheets before Googling *how to delete
your search history*. They do not kiss the cinnamon
whiskey lips of their best friend at a party, run their fingers
through her long, sunbeam hair before she goes home
with her boyfriend. They do not check out each other's butts—
even though *all* your girlfriends say its normal
for girls to check out each other's butts.

Those girls are probably writing other versions
of this poem right now—but that's beside the point.

Baby, you are gay—and not as in happy. You won't
be that for awhile, but you are gay as in queer
as fuck. As in one day, your face will be on a flier
on the bathroom door at the queer bar, hair blazing
fuchsia. As in one day your wedding will feature

a board labeled *The Gay Agenda* and your friends
will cheer when you kiss a handsome
woman in a black wedding dress. As in one day
you will feel bad for your straight friends because
they're just *so* boring. As in one day you will work
at a mechanic shop decorated with pronoun pins
and pride. As in one day your partners will write poems
or songs about you. As in one day *family* will mean
more coveted collective than anything you were born
with. As in one day you will be so happy.

Polyamory Throws a Party

Polyamory rearranges the tables
into one long parade, adds extra
seats for plus ones, plus twos,
or plus fours. She adds velvet
couches draped in satiny blankets,
puffy pillows. She gowns herself
in sequins, irises glow glitter
as she greets everyone
by name. Champagne twinkles
into flutes while guests gush
over their partner's partners.
Polyamory's whole
body pulses pink as her cheeks
as she watches the people she loves
surrounded by the love they deserve.

I AM TOO MUCH FOR MOST

I tried to shove my too much into my pocket,
forearms straining as I struggled to smash

her between my palms until she burst into sequins—
a confetti crime scene. My too much crowned

herself Queen, superglued rhinestones to a scepter,
put on a parade and sneezed pink boa feathers

for weeks after. She spends hours color-coordinating
selfies she sends to each of my partners so no one forgets

what she looks like. She asks
doyoulikemedoyoulikemedoyoulikemedoyoulike

music? She only gets that last part out
because everyone loves   music.

She wore glitter
pumps to my book release,

and when the boy made of sandpaper
didn't come, she cried until she grew a tail

and swam in the saltiest sea. She lives in the hollow
behind my voice box, twists around the tiny tendrils

of all the times I've ever been
alone. Sometimes I forget to breathe.

My too much is the color the sun stings.
When I put her in water

she sprouts arms and legs and introduces
herself to the people I am trying to date.

I am always surrounded by an ocean
of my own undoing. Ex-lovers have labeled her

unlovable. I have conflated the two in my head.
When I try to lock my too much in a closet

she reminds me I've already ripped
that door off its hinges. She won't stop telling

every new person I meet how queer
and polyamorous I am like it's a personality trait.

She printed out a picture of my ass and nailed it
to the bedroom wall. My wife reminds me

we're not the only people we invite into the bedroom
and both me and my too much grin

because we never half-ass anything,
and I've got my whole ass on the wall to prove it.

Albert Ellis and I Explore His Theories on Catastrophic Thinking

He says *they don't love you and never will.*
No *what if,* he makes it a fact.

At first I fight it—there's no evidence,
just my brain's casual cruise
to the worst case scenario.

He calls this *catastrophizing*—suggests we *lean
into it.* I search his curious, unrelenting
eyes, and my chest shrugs a bloated sigh as I shrink

into this reality. Then I've wasted my love
poems. He quips *okay—you've wasted*

your poems. Now what? I explain I have collected
paper trails of the places my heart has wandered
alone, infatuated with anticipation.

There is a catalog of honey-drenched
language, soft lips—words that have planted
themselves onto twitterpated leaves.

Maybe I'm a garden.
Maybe my poems are seeds.

But I don't want to be a metaphor.

Then what are you?
he inquires. I am stripped
bare in the way they say to imagine

everyone naked when giving a speech,
but then all I can picture is myself naked
in a room full of penises—I mean people

I love that don't love me.
              (freudian slip)

He says *that's still a metaphor.*

So maybe I am a metaphor, but
I don't want to be where things don't grow

from. Maybe I am naked.
I have tattooed my blushed
affections onto my sleeve. I won't wait
an extra day to text back, in fact, I'll send voice
messages while I'm driving home from a date.
I will only arrange bouquets flowered
with *love-me* engraved petals.
What I'm trying to say is

I have nothing
to hide.

And maybe she won't love me.
And maybe he'll be smitten
by my clumsy displays
showcasing the ways I've been falling.

Either way,
I'm still going to write love poems.
Still going to slip lipstick
prints into the pockets of the people I love
that might not love me back. If love echoes,
reflects back to only my ears, and *this* is the worst
case scenario, then I'll wave valentine
verses into an ocean—pen handwritten
love letters on every wall. I'll make it easy to find,
illuminated in the soft glow of a pink neon sign.

Self Portrait as Someone to Love

after Megan Falley

She's too pretty for plain coffee
or matching clothes. She scares children
with her cackling, and she is the funniest
person she knows. She bought gold
pens with swappable ink to write love letters
to her friends in multicolor like a mood ring.
Patron Saint of Everything Pink. She has a room
dedicated to poetry, mauve chaise in the corner
for the dramatics. She swears all the time
and fucking hates squirrels. Her mother calls her
poems cute, but a little *too* intimate. She falls
up the stairs, flashes her lover's neighbors—
insists on short skirts. She hangs pictures
of herself naked throughout the house
to remind her she's someone worth fucking,
and the only bush she beats around is her own.
She's a Virgo sun with a Leo moon
so she's a gavel-toting-cheerleader-bisexual-
queen, red gel pen and eyebrows raised,
writing 5-star reviews with praise and accolades.
She is lemon-sour anticipation,
the way she coats your teeth. Douses herself
in glitter, smells of kerosene. She falls
over furniture, wakes up with bruises
she cannot recall what from. She curates playlists
based on her vocal range, lies about not knowing
how to sing. She names her pets and plants
after people she doesn't want to meet. She drinks

wine a bottle at a time and texts bad poetry
to her partner about their eyes. She has a thing
for musicians who like spreadsheets.
She is the funniest person her therapist knows,
or at least pretends to be to say she's won
at therapy. She designed a seventy-two step bedtime
routine that begins sprawled out on the chaise,
lamenting about the seventy-one steps left
to go. She once called her period a murder-mystery
machine, swoons over extravagance, tapes
rainbow streamers to the kitchen door. She falls
in love with everything *extra*, says *thank you*
and curtsies when anyone labels her *too much*—
she would never settle for *only* being enough.

Acknowledgments

I am so grateful to the editors of the following journals and anthologies, in which these pieces, some of them in slightly different versions, first appeared:

Rat's Ass Review: "Her Lover's Teeth Leave a Bruise"

Quartz Literary: "Polyamory from the Perspective of an Anniversary Card"

Beyond the Veil Press: "Dear Poet"

Boats Against the Current: "Hands"

South Broadway Ghost Society: "What's Left," and "Another Period Poem"

Moss Puppy Magazine: "Humane"

Last Leaves Magazine: "While Cleaning Out My Underwear Drawer I Wondered When All My Underwear Became Period Underwear"

Twenty Bellows: "Albert Ellis and I Explore His Theories on Catastrophic Thinking," "Schrödinger's Heart," and "My Dating Situation Has Gotten So Disappointing that My Wife is Trying to Give Me Dating Advice"

In addition, "I AM TOO MUCH FOR MOST" was published and nominated for the Best of the Net Award in 2023 by *Gnashing Teeth Publishing.*

"Cannibal, or My Boyfriend Dumped Me Before I Finished Writing this Poem" was a finalist for the 2023 Joy Bale Boone prize, and published in *The Heartland Review.*

"the one about the girl and the closet" was a finalist for the Bellingham Review 2024 Literary Contest, and published in *Bellingham Review.*

Thank You

I owe a huge thank you to everyone who has helped make this book possible. This was no small feat, and I had so much support along the way.

Thank you Connor Wolfe and Wayfarer Books for believing in this book and its message and helping me share it. I am so grateful to be part of a press that is forging a path to a better and more inclusive world.

Thank you Megan Falley for being the most tender poetry teacher and word magician. You helped me fall in love with poetry and all the things I can create with it. I am immensely grateful to you for creating Poems that Don't Suck and cultivating the incredible community that stemmed from it.

Thank you Diane Lato and all of the other folks who spent hours pouring over all of my drafts and helping me edit and mold these poems into what they were meant to be.

Thank you Britta Hurula for loving so many different versions of me over the last twelve years. I am so lucky to be loved by you. Thank you for letting me share some of our secrets with the whole world, and encouraging me to be my whole self.

Thank you Nic Morrison for loving and celebrating all of my too much. You are in so much of this book—not just the poems about you, but also in the poems about learning to love myself. Thank you for being so easy to love.

Thank you Deirdre McGrath for reading all my poems, even when they're a little too intimate. I hope I grow up to be as open to learning and growing as you are.

Thank you Becca, Megan, Maple, Nic, Kevin, Kelly, Marissa and the rest of the Denver poetry community for creating a beautiful space to share and create.

Thank you Sage Herrin and Beyond the Veil Press for giving me a home and place to share the joy I've found in poetry.

Thank you Patricia Smith, Jared Singer, Jay Ward, Siaara Freeman, Victoria Chang, and Patrick Roche for holding space in workshops where a lot of these poems were created.

Thank you Becca for being my poetry partner and for being someone I look up to on and off the page.

Thank you Kelly for sharing a brain with me and celebrating all of my successes. I'm so glad you asked to meet up and write together. My life and my poetry are better because of you.

Thank you Sundress Publications and the SAFTA Residency Program at Firefly Farms for giving me a space where this book first took shape and transformed from an idea and a few pages of poems to a fully realized book.

about the author

Tyler Hurula (she/they) is the pinkest poet and explorer based in Denver, Colorado. She strives to be the most queer and polyamorous person they can be. You'll likely find her parading around in a tiara with hot pink lipstick going to an art walk, writing at a coffee shop, or discussing the intricacies of the latest horror movie she's watched with anyone who will listen. They enjoy reading poetry out loud to their two cats and chihuahua named Poet (after her). Author of chapbook *Love Me Louder* (Querencia Press). Their poems can be found in publications including *Anti-Heroin Chic*, *South Broadway Press*, *Boats Against the Current*, *Gnashing Teeth Publishing*, and more. They have been nominated for Best of the Net and Pushcart Prizes, and was a finalist for the Write Bloody 2024 Jack McCarthy Book Prize Contest. You can find her on Instagram @theprettypinkpoet and online at tylerhurula.com.

SINCE 2012

At Wayfarer Books we believe poetry is the language of the earth. We believe words—shaped like rivers through wild places—can change the shape of the world. We publish poets and writers and renegades who stand outside of mainstream culture—poets, essayists, and storytellers whose work might withstand the scrutiny of crows and coyotes, those who are cryptic and floral, the crepuscular, and the queer-at-heart. We are more than just a publisher but a community of writers. Our mission is to produce books that can serve as a compass and map to all wayfarers through wild terrain.

wayfarerbooks.org